# Dark Moon Light

## Discovering Your World with Magic, Mysticism, and the Paranormal

Written by Lauren Hellekson

Illustrations by Audrey Henry

# Dedications

*For my coven. Farrah, Jess, and Rachel. I've always had the breath of magic within me, but you showed me how to truly breathe.*

*My husband Christopher, the first man to call me a witch with love, excitement, and pride. I love you for eternity.*

*And to you, my dear reader, I hope these pages bring you curiosity, magic, courage, and empowerment. Believe that you are everything you need to be for this very moment.*

*I am so glad you're here....*

*-L*

# Table of Contents

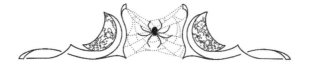

If by picking up this book, you're expecting to learn how to hex your partner's mother, cast demons out of your next haunt, or find out which deity wants you to be their high priest/priestess, do I have some news for you! Those lofty goals won't be found within these pages and I'm in a place spiritually that I am ok with being the target of your disappointment.

However, I urge you to continue forward as there are many paths to this journey, and you may find yourself doing far greater work than a measly spell to make the ol' monster-in-law lose her teeth. (Although, if you're lucky, I'll write another book on just that. But I digress.) This piece of literature is a tool to help you open your mind, your heart, and your spirit to the already mystical world around you. To help uncover the gifts that are right at your fingertips. To encourage you to infuse every waking moment with your intuition, as well as theory, ceremony, intention, and power. In writing this book I aim to help you awaken magic that is already inside of you.

So, who the heck am I? That's a great question considering

you've put enough faith in me to pick up my book. To detail the amount of time I've been practicing witchcraft, spirituality, and energy work would be a much more in-depth answer than what's applicable here, as I believe those who are called to this life have been practicing most of our lives. The formal timeline of me openly sharing my practice is much more condensed and appropriate here.

So, let's start from the beginning, shall we? I'm sure all modern witches can relate to the Wicca phase as teens ... Who else got in trouble for drawing a pentagram on the hardwood floors in their bedroom? Just me? I was a wild teen, I had (and still have) a lot of trauma I'm forever sorting through, and, at the time, I was using rebellion as a coping mechanism.

After that, I spent a couple of years deep in a "Christian phase" where my interest in biblical mythology grew and ultimately led to being pushed away (or according to the congregation, I fell) from that belief system. Then, in adulthood, turned into the "quirky", suit wearing, corporate ladder climber with an unhealthy love for whiskey. Alcohol helped me to suppress a lot of work that was key to my spiritual growth. One of the biggest takeaways I've learned from the journey that I'm on is: you really should feel everything safely. I deeply believe in modern medicine and taking care of yourself professionally when needed. Taking advantage of what we have access to in a modern world can be paramount to living a healthy, safe, and magical existence. Be wary of those who tell you otherwise.

Caring for yourself with modern means is modern magic. Addiction, however, is not and should not be part of that process.

The path that led me into open spirituality came several years ago when I dropped the almost 6 figure corporate gig and opened a business (I was in a very privileged place to be able to take that journey, I would never suggest reckless life changes). It was the first time I took a hard turn from most of the advice I was being given and deviated from a "practical path".

In my new business venture, I employed someone who was a beautiful but very tortured soul. They also suffered from addiction, and it ended up taking their life at a very young age. A spiritual practice was part of their journey to wellness and healing and that stuck with me. I closed that business shortly after and moved away from my hometown, eventually landing myself in India, inspired to learn about the practices they were trying so hard to find healing through. I spent time exploring and learning and receiving certifications in yogic practices and meditation.

That curiosity turned into a thirst, further leading me to the mystical hillsides and cliffs of Ireland, the churches and holy lands of Israel, the healing and mineral rich waters of the Dead Sea, and many other adventures in the name of finding that spark, that missing piece I needed to bring healing to both myself, and those still on this earth who don't have the means or access to drop their life and hop on a plane. This deviation from my life as it was, brought around my own sobriety, and it blossomed into a community of healing. I opened a yoga asana practice space in my hometown and spent a few years sharing with people what a spiritual practice can open up within them.

During this time was when the world was hit with one of the worst pandemics in recent history. We were all tested, pushed to the edge, were shown who we could trust and who truly cared about their follow man. We lost so many humans during that time, and as a business that dealt in the health and wellbeing of the community, we lost a lot. Financially the studio never fully recovered and ended up closing. In hindsight, the outcome of that venture was inevitable. Being a yogic educator as a white woman in the west, was always going to be a short-lived endeavor, as that practice wasn't for me to continue educating with. I still very much use yogic teachings, history, and practices in my healing modalities, in a way that honors and respects what I have learned, but I no longer connect to the western community of that practice, and I feel I may never have.

Although the studio ran its course to completion over a span of about 6 years, it was during its life that I was called to begin educating those who were interested in craft work and expanding their spiritual practice. In hindsight, this path had always been waiting for me as this was when my beautiful coven was born along with the blossoming of my confidence, power, and ability. From there, I began group workshops about beginner craft, started expanding my own practice, and became more open and prouder of who I was.

I joined a paranormal investigation team in 2022 after about 14 years of solo investigation and started using my knowledge, abilities, and teaching methods to share applicable practices in the paranormal world. You'll notice that I'll be going back and forth between witchcraft and other paranormal work, specifically investigation.

When figuring out exactly why I wanted to write this book, I was doing so from a point in my life where I felt complete in where I was working spiritually. Heavily practicing witchcraft, while also being a paranormal investigator gives me such a deep and satisfying balance that it has really helped me to feel both grounded and powerful. It is such an integral piece of who I am both as a witch and as a researcher that it felt only right to bring this information to you in a way that could potentially help those from either, or both worlds.

I remember a few years ago, when I first tried to practice in front of another person. I pretended to have no idea what was going on and allowed them to teach me, gauge my own methods and see if it was "doing it correctly". Being open publicly was difficult for me because for most of my adult life, I constantly needed validation from others. Whether it was the validation of being cool, loved, unique, intelligent etc. I never really stood on my own authentically...until now.

I'm still so new to this life out in the open, and the feeling of being lost, alone, and unseen is still so fresh. I don't want anyone to feel the exclusion that I once felt, and I hope this book also aids in that.

I hope it serves you well.

# Introduction

Society tends to use the term "witchcraft" as a blanket term for many things. It's root word "witch" in and of itself is over a thousand years old. We often associate witchcraft with things throughout western mainstream culture; whether it's popular and dark television shows about teen sorcerers, movies featuring outcast occult high schoolers, popularized religious sects of craft with strong symbolism and rules of three, or historical tragedies in history where the word was used to demonize, torture, and murder marginalized people. The term is not something any of us must think very hard about to form an opinion.

So, what really is the root of this practice? Or more specifically this idea that we have a power or control over the unseen energies of the universe? We may think there is this straight line through history of how witchcraft made its way through time, but it's only that simple if we look at the practice with a more European/Christian centered perspective. From a world view, that question really has endless answers. From the

Mangkukulam of the Philippines, the Machi women of Chile or the practice of Obeah in Haiti, the concept of manipulating the energies of nature, the universe, and beyond is by no means a new concept. People are still being persecuted today for "witchcraft". Their communities and cultures are oppressed by the use of that word making it harmful and dangerous. That's a fact that is incredibly important to consider and not to be taken lightly when entering this world. Being a witch and using that word to describe yourself must always be a conscious and thoughtful commitment. It is a label you choose yourself and only you can make that decision.

When thinking about mainstream witchcraft, particularly in the west, it tends to focus on practices of Wicca, Pagan/neo-Pagan beliefs, Greek Mythology, and Christian Mythology. However, the practice isn't just limited to those who have a specific religious or belief system. It wouldn't make sense to go from atheism to deity work or using Roman Catholic imagery. Practitioners can "believe" in craft work, energy, healing, manifesting, and the power of this ever-expanding universe without needing the structure of religion. There are ways we can develop a practice without the theology aspect and that's a great starting point for everyone. Your practice can build up and around core values of self-awareness, acknowledgement, research, and patience.

The idea that we can make things happen for ourselves with just our thoughts, some exotic (and albeit scary or odd) ingredients is usually what we take from stories of spells, meant to hex an enemy or conjure fame and fortune for oneself. Witchcraft, in reality, is as simple as working together with the energy, both spiritual and universal, that is around and inside of you, in order to be able to see the possibilities your environment is blossoming with. Do I think printing out a picture of somebody to hex them is going to hurt them? No (you need a little more than that). Do I think that a money jar can encourage, commit, and motivate a change in your financial outcome? Yes. Most times, it takes just a little bit of magic to show ourselves what we're capable of. When we allow our minds to believe the magic is real, we're a little less likely to doubt ourselves and we become far more motivated to accomplish things we never thought were possible. We might apply for that position that we think we're underqualified for because we performed a new moon ceremony. Perhaps, we reach out to that person that we've had a crush on because we did a love spell. Sometimes magic is the excuse we need to realize that we are the magic.

Do I also think that it's more than that? Absolutely.

How can modern world witches identify with a practice that spans across global culture and centuries of history? Typically, practices are handed down through generations of family magic. However, when you're coming into this as a first-generation witch, it can be daunting. What we must realize though, is first generation witches are full of possibility. This is where tradition starts. Where stories begin. Where generations of witches follow. First generation witches are an integral part of the future of magic. Be mindful though, every new adventure must be accompanied by a warning; there are still many ways in which we can harm unintentionally as we develop our craft.

While you discover your calling within this work, there will be many things that seem interesting, special, or exciting. However, not everything will be for you. Some magic is deeply rooted in very specific cultures. While it may be frustrating being told that you're not allowed to have something, it's not because you're not worthy, but because those practices won't work for you in the way they're intended. When we try to force ourselves into places or practices that aren't meant for us, we can damage those energies for the people that do and are supposed to work with them.

The topic of cultural appropriation in witchcraft is such a huge and important piece of starting this journey. Being an adopted, white, French, European person I will do my best to encourage and nudge you in the direction of figuring out and honoring ways that you can start your practice appropriately. If by chance you share in my European lineal descent, I urge you to listen and hear the black, indigenous, people of color, and other marginalized communities, outside of your immediate circle, when it comes to practices that are considered closed. Most starting points you find with me will be based around intuition, exploration, and an encouragement to research further on your own.

Witchcraft isn't a one size fits all practice, as we all come from different cultures, lines of thinking, and individual belief systems. To tell you that there's one way to practice would be irresponsible. This craft, at its core, has likely been practiced far longer than documented. I will always choose to teach from the path of setting a sturdy foundation of physical, emotional, and spiritual awareness and acknowledgement. Observation and exploration of your immediate surroundings. Using your environment and things that you already have access to. Respect and research of items, practices, and methods found amongst mainstream channels.

Witchcraft should feel and be inclusive. You don't have to be rich, have access to a specialty occult shop, or own a $6,000 cauldron to be a witch. Your crafting ability, potency, and progression can be obtained equally from a thrift store stock pot. When it comes to this kind of inclusivity, you may be told otherwise. You may be told that very specific and often expensive items are crucial to do certain things. This is a false narrative based in classist ideology and very much a red flag. At the end of the day, we are the magic.

While you may find suggestions or general lists of optional things to have on hand within these pages, it's not to say any of it is needed to start a practice. There are plenty of ways to live a magical life without purchasing anything beyond what you can find within your immediate reach, in nature, or within your own energy. Historically, we must think about what humans had access to. What they could make, gather, and forage on their own was what was used for craft work. Don't get me wrong, I love stocking my pantry and cabinets with herbs, candles, tools, and collectables, but that doesn't make me a witch. My proclamation, patience, dedication, and acknowledgment; honoring the moon, my body, my emotions, and my loved ones; being kind and mindful to the earth and her energies; and most of all, being kind to myself are all the things that together, make me a witch.

What next? That's the most important question you should always take the time to ask yourself. When we stumble, change our mind, learn something new, educate ourselves in something we need to unlearn, work through our mistakes, and figure out how to grow around them. The only thing that matters, is what we do next. As for now, read through these pages, practice the exercises, write in your journal, try the crafty activities. If you're currently in the paranormal community, allow this to open more avenues for new investigative techniques, and to further hone your intuitiveness. This isn't meant to turn you into a witch, but just to encourage you to realize that creating a magical life isn't unreasonable. That it's ok to dream, hope, and plan. That even the mundane can be beautiful, bountiful, and intentional. You are already everything you need to be in this moment, and this is only to help guide you to the door, show you the handle, and encourage you to open it.

The rest is up to you.

Let's get started

# Chapter One

*I'm Always a witch but.........*

1.5  2.5  10  20+

I've often been asked as an educator how embracing witchcraft and practicing witchcraft helps in areas of the paranormal. Paranormal investigative and practicing craft worlds are so deeply related but we seldom see the correlation at first. If you are or want to be a practicing witch, and you're interested in the paranormal, this is a great segue into that world. On the other hand, if as a paranormal investigator, you want to find some deeper exploration practices, protection methods, or if you have, in the past, used experimental techniques, hopefully this will bring you some additional guidance and encourage you to continue thinking outside the box. This is truly where we as investigators should want to live.

I am always a witch, but I am first and foremost an investigator, researcher, and enthusiast of the paranormal. We often hear this term "paranormal investigator" and immediately think "BRO! It's a demon!". However, when we step away from the entertainment industry, and instead break down the language, the prefix para- has a multitude of meanings. In the case of paranormal, it means "beyond", or beyond the normal.

Like most in this field, the afterlife, unknown, mystical, and all the interworking of spiritual energy throughout the universe has fascinated me since my childhood. My mother once told me about an imaginary friend I used to have named, Ducky. She always assumed it was a duck and I constantly talked about him being with me at school, and with us in the car. One day after preschool, (that was housed in a historic church no less) she asked where Ducky was and I simply replied, "Oh, he got to go home" and she never heard about him again. Small happenings like this are always reasons to think, was there more there?

Into my adolescence, I remember my dad letting me borrow his shoulder mount Panasonic camcorder to make movies, that eventually led to documenting the spooky happenings around our home. In my early teens, I remember exploring his apartment complex in a historic building. Then of course finding the "plumbers by day, ghost hunters by night" 2004 premier of Ghost Hunters, further solidifying my interest in the paranormal. Then in my early 20s, in my first apartment, I had my first concrete, documented, experience in the over 100-year-old complex.

Being a primarily solo investigator for most of my experience, the fear factor of that work was heightened. This led me to combine my practices from the occult into my rituals before exploration. When I would use symbols, smoke clear my equipment, or even just wear something that I made to keep myself grounded, it always resulted in feeling an extra layer of protection, that would in turn, keep me focused and objective.

When we talk about energy, witchcraft, protection, etc., we are talking about the paranormal. We can surmise this as we are technically working with the same ideas, methods, and practices that are otherwise beyond our scope of what is considered "normal". Thus, when making your craft an everyday practice, you're also bringing the paranormal into everyday practice. This correlation changes how we see beyond the waking world and allows us to interact, in many ways, with energy outside of our typical scope of practice.

Typically, those who are part of this "beyond normal" world, tend to want to know everything that's out there. Whether or not paranormal investigation is on your plate of activities that you would like to explore, practicing craft related techniques could help bring an analytical value to your investigative approach. That may sound like a contradiction, but when we become more familiar with what we're looking for and how to feel for it because we're working with similar energy, it can help us to discern what are plausible experiences verses fear or excitement-based speculation. Think of it like building immunity, when we flood our immune system with antigens to create antibodies, we heighten our immune system. In the same way, we can build a heightened awareness regarding paranormal energy and have a more critical viewpoint of it. This idea and practice can also aid in protection practices, cleansing, and keeping your energy safe.

Especially if you find yourself often in haunted lunatic asylums, prisons, or hospitals, like I do.

Some great crafty methods to bring to your next hunt include: Protection crystals: especially if you connect with the mystic minerals as a way to feel grounded and prepared. Make sure you have a cleansing practice in place to both clear and recharge your stones between haunts.

Equipment sigils: (you can find sigil making in the "Recipes" section of this book); I have a protection symbol on my gear case, and I always make sure to say a prayer or incantation over my equipment, especially my batteries (if you know, you know).

Amulets or protective items that you can wear on your person: witches salt (also found in the "Recipes" section) in jewelry, ancestor items, or other wearables always help me to feel calm and aware.

You can also use practices like communication via dowsing rods, pendulums, or mediums. Just remember that these are considered more subjective approaches and should be used sparingly. Don't let methods without an outside source for validation lead the investigation. When you're gathering evidence, you have to focus on things that are documentable. Crossing copper or receiving messages from beyond won't always hold up analytically, but they can add some extra pizazz to the case file as a whole.

Techniques like these can, however, be combined with documentable approaches like atmospheric or environment changes. These changes can be measured with equipment that most investigators either use or have heard of.

- Radiating Electromagnetic Field devices, or REM pods, will emit their own fields of energy and are theorized to be easily manipulatable by the unseen with just their immediate presence around the device.
- Thermal imaging is an even more reliable method of recording changes in the atmosphere's temperature. Theoretically, the presence of spirit energy will cause fluctuations in temperature without explanation.

When we're dealing with fields that can be so deeply manipulated by our feelings, emotions, opinions, and personal beliefs, it will always be a balancing act to stay grounded, secure and safe.

There's this misconception that "witchy" people are versed in ghost hunting, and ghost hunters know all about occult practices. This, surprisingly, couldn't be further from the truth. Have I met plenty of very knowledgeable folks who balance these worlds appropriately? Absolutely. At the risk of sounding egomaniacal, I'd like to say that I've worked very hard to be one of those people. Have I made my companions pocket crystals before going into those extra questionable locations? Yes. But in my defense, nobody's been possessed thus far.

Some of my personal code of conduct while investigating,

whether as a witch or not, is always enter a space with Respect, Compassion, and Professionalism. It's so easy to fall into bad habits in the paranormal world. We're surrounded by productions and celebrities that need you to feel entertained even if it's at the risk of misinformation. Of course, it's the paranormal, it's essentially an entirely unexplained genre. However, that doesn't mean it should be a free for all.

Respect your surroundings. This goes for locations, energy, and people both among us and otherwise not on the same plain of existence. Keep the on-site practice of witchcraft out of the investigation. This includes ceremonies, summoning, even cleansing a space without a direct request of the homeowner or owner of the space to elicit activity or evidence. Doing so is incredibly disrespectful.

Have Compassion for how you may affect the spaces you occupy. This includes but is not limited to, avoiding negative provocation, "crossing over" without consent, and speculating undocumented history.

Carry Professionalism like a badge. Every interaction with energy that is not your own should be met with an impartial and objective attitude. Don't invite anything into your body, home, or to go anywhere with you. Focus on the task, accumulation of evidence, and take appropriate action on a case-by-case basis.

When putting these practices to work, don't forget to also check the ego at the door. The majority of investigative practices should consist mostly of observation. When we want to overtake any situation, especially with our emotions or projections, we can sometimes create the risk of causing more damage than good. In addition, we also miss out on potential information and communication. Use this same logic in your magical practice as well. Observe, absorb, and record before you react and respond.

# Chapter Two

*Don't focus the beginning of your journey*

*on what "kind" of witch you are....*

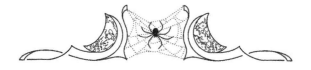

One of the more controversial things I like to point out when educating is; even Catholics dabble in the occult. Burning incense, hanging bags of herbs over doors, quietly invoking guidance from deities, invoking with books of sacred texts. It's all there, and yet, the fear, guilt, and judgement passed on to practitioners outside the church is devastating.

When we take this theological methodology into the paranormal world as a whole, we run into a lot of problematic assumptions. We generalize, place labels, and have a default recommendation of using religious means to explain or remedy the situation. This, in my albeit brash opinion, is incredibly myopic and irresponsible. It's human nature to need answers, to explore, discover and explain the unknown. When we disregard the evolution of science as an ever-expanding and growing area of study and limit the ideas, methods, and research in the paranormal world, we can end up with a plethora of evidence that's dismissed on account of archaic thinking.

When we decide to have a more broad, universal, and

energetic centered approach in an investigative world, we can use our craft, awareness, and introspection to our advantage. Our crafting is both explorative and analytical. It requires deep thought and observation. It also requires us to sometimes take things exactly for what they are, and to not insert our beliefs or inflate the situation. The point here is, don't limit your practice or your belief process, and be open to new developments in your experiences, thoughts, feelings, and life. Humans are wonderers and wanderers; those are worthy things to embrace.

When it comes to our personal power in faith and belief, it's important to be firm in your convictions, for yourself. When I speak about the damage of "Christ" based faiths to the occult community, it's not to damn, or dismiss the Christian faith. I have close friends and companions who I see as Christ-like. There is a difference. Deity wise, I have a special place for Yeshua in my development as a witch.

Christian mythology has played a heavy role in the history and formation of certain ideas in the occult and the paranormal in general. This "demon" centered system declares that witchcraft is evil, that energy that presents itself in 3s is "mocking a trinity", or that you must use a priest to cleanse and "exorcise" evil from your life. These ideas regarding witchcraft specifically, are instilled as part of an over 500-year-old feud between the Catholic and Protestant belief systems. Believe it or not, from 900 to the early 1400s witchcraft wasn't even acknowledged, let alone punished. In fact, in the mid 1200s, Pope Alexander IV publicly stated that punishing witchcraft would not be tolerated. As soon as the mid 1300s however, safety from the church was dissolved as yet another Pope, ol' Greg the 6th, declared all magic was done with the aid of demons and thus was prosecutable as heresy. The biggest blow came with the 1486 publication of, "Malleus Maleficarum", or "The Hammer of Witches". This misogynistic handbook where witchcraft was solely blamed on women, was centered around the biblical passage in the book of Exodus, "Thou shalt not suffer a witch to live". However, the accuracy of the original Hebrew word, mekhashepha, being translated to "witch", has been widely debated as the book of Exodus was written thousands of years ago. This momentum led to the accusation, torture, and murder of countless lives. Most of whom very likely never had practiced witchcraft. When we glamourize this history or reinforce the label that was otherwise a death sentence to those who lost their lives, we're disrespecting ancestorial energy. As stated before, the term "witch" isn't to be given to those who are not able to be part of that conversation. It was a tactic of oppression and still is for many cultures.

Rather than religious belief systems explaining the supernatural, perhaps it's that the supernatural is instead deeply rooted in the birth and formation of these religious beliefs. Just like the over 10,000 different religions found globally, you will also find many types of magical craft. Don't focus the beginning of your journey on what "kind" of witch you are or want to be. Not only will that make you feel boxed in, but there is also no way to take a quick quiz or answer a few questions and be told exactly who you are as a person, so why should it work for your craft? Be open, willing, and sometimes experimental with how you lay your path ahead. Try new things, be conscious of where those things are coming from and if they're generally meant for you, and you will be able to forge your own path without labels, religion, or internet sorting quizzes.

There are probably so many things we already do in our day to day that stem from ritualistic practices. Opening up and noticing these things, can help to bring more awareness, and intention to how we're conducting these actions and how we conduct ourselves. Your craft can be practiced while you're making dinner, taking a bath, grocery shopping, hiking, even at the office. The more we immerse our mundane tasks in witchcraft, the more we normalize a magical life, and in turn, the more we expect from ourselves and our surroundings. We then start to connect with the power that is now within our reach. Starting today, be conscious and aware of your daily activities. How do your mornings go? Do you have a specific morning beverage or snack, a regular routine throughout your living space? Even a chaotic morning with other humans can be ritualistic (believe it or not). Find your flow, your habits, the things that work for you and start to really acknowledge and lean into those things. Sometimes seeing the chaos, the spilled coffee, the extra red lights on the way to work, all have a purpose we can give them. They can all be useful for us. This is not to be confused with the typical "give it to god" trope, but more so taking ownership of the things that sometimes feel out of our control. Standing in our power. Bad things happen and that's a truth we cannot deny. However, when we stand in our power for those small inconvenient moments and we don't allow them to pull our peace away from us, we gain strength and resilience that will help us conquer future moments where we want to fall.

We tend to create this specific picture of what being a witch looks like in our minds. From the clothing to the home, to all the fancy eclectic items they surround themselves with. Something I will never stress enough is how important it is not to expect or strive for a pin worthy aesthetic when it comes to starting your craft. Although visually pleasing, you will limit what you can do and explore because you will focus on the material aspects rather than the practice itself. The only magic this "material forward" thinking will create will be the demise and disappearing act of your practice itself. Witchcraft can be unorganized, mismatched, it can be cheap, poorly written, still have spaghetti sauce labels on it. That's ok. The only thing your craft needs to be, is yours.

Grab a notebook and a writing utensil. Step away from this book for a moment and walk around your house/apartment/ living space. Make a list, and then use tick marks and record the following:

- Empty jars
- Knick knacks that don't have any real purpose other than you liked them, so you put them on a shelf (rocks, old nails, small versions of things, figurines, broken items, etc.)
- Books you haven't read that you solely bought for the cover
- An overabundance of one specific type of thing: plants, rocks, glass like ocean glass, beads, bones, types of art, sticks, etc.

If you have even a small list, you're taking inventory of your tools. As a witch, you will be called to your pantry of magical items. One thing the stereotypes got right about us; we all have the possibility of being the witch in the woods with the gloriously cluttered cottage full of our crafty items. Your list may seem silly at first, but when you start to see your world as a witch, their properties and use will open to you. There is a presence that is important when we're doing works of a magical nature. The need to be in the exact moment that we're crafting, focusing, manifesting, or setting intention directly coincides with the potency of that particular activity. Just like any project, when we're heavily distracted, it takes away from the quality of work rather than when we're focused, present, and engaged. This is another quality that I find in investigating the paranormal as well. When there are impatient, or otherwise distracted investigators, they're always the first to jump up and down at any sign of a creaky floorboard or energy fluctuation. They're seeing what they want to see, and not what is actually there. While we do need a little faith, imagination, and to really believe in what we're doing, we can still approach the magical world from an analytic perspective. This might sound like an oxymoron, and I understand that. However, before great scientific discoveries, wasn't the explanation similar? Isn't it all just a little magic after all?

I want you to go back through that list you made about the items around your space. There's an acknowledgement that needs to happen when we transition our mundane surrounding into a magical one. Although it may feel silly, try walking around your space again, touch each individual item and express that it is a tool with a purpose that will be revealed to you. What we are doing here, is creating a dialogue with the energy that may have brought these items to you. The more we have this awareness towards the material items in our lives, the more we can discern what needs to be used in our practice, and what needs to be let go. Whether these items eventually need to be given back to the earth, or you just don't need them anymore, cleaning your space is just as much a magical practice as filling it.

This exercise of taking inventory helps with both of those things. We either connect with an item, or we know in our being that it does not or will not serve us and the act of letting it go has a deep and powerful magic to it. This act of cleaning or cleansing will come up a lot in your practice. There are times throughout our human existence, whether it's connected to lunar phases, seasons, or the days of the week that we'll be called to cleanse, and release what is not serving us, and this is an integral part of becoming one with the cycle of creation. A cycle we must partake in to have access to the energies of the universe. Only then can we connect with that power and harness it to aid in our work.

The full cycle of something is so important to its progression. Allowing everything to complete its cycle is paramount to a magical existence. That cycle of creation consists of birth, life, death. This is prevalent in all things we experience. Not only in the obvious ways of being born of this earth and one day returning to it, but also in the things that surround us. The connections we make with other humans, animals, objects, projects, jobs, hobbies, and so on. These things all have a beginning when the connection is "born". A life span, sometimes a brief moment, sometimes much longer. And ultimately, they will all have an end. There's a deep importance to that part of the cycle as the end is the only way room can be made for more growth, more creation, and more connection. Since energy is never actually created, nor destroyed, we must actively partake in this cycle for the energy we're trying to work from, to become part of us. Think of this idea like a generator. The more we can actively work within this process, the more we can access the energy of the universe. So, try not to hoard...materially, spiritually, emotionally. You'll run out of space for all the new growth you will be experiencing.

I firmly believe when it comes to encouraging our own growth, it's important to meet ourselves exactly where we are. To see what is there, and not necessarily what we want to be there. On any journey, but especially on those of a more spiritual and energetic nature, we can often fall into a few different distractions that have the potential to lead to more harmful practices or veer us off track completely.

One that I find the easiest to fall into is what is known as destination addiction. The idea that our growth, happiness, success, etc. is somewhere that we're not. I've seen this in almost every line of work that I've been in. It was most prevalent during my time as a trainer/fitness coach but is still very much present in the spiritual community as well. If you find yourself pressing hard for what's next, or saying statements like, "I'll be happier if I can just get to this point", then you're focusing on the next moment rather than the one you're in. Do we have to find happiness in everything? No. It's ok to acknowledge and feel some of the less happy emotions. Sometimes feeling exactly where we are can help in understanding what we need to do next. We can become more productive instead of trying to live beyond the exact place where we are right now.

This is not to be mistaken with the idea that we can "Choose happiness!" as that too falls under another distraction that we'll discuss. Destination addiction steals the happiness we are capable of feeling because it tells us that we could be better, do better, and have more if we just _____. That's where the addiction lies.

Becoming connected and aware of your surroundings, tools, space, collection habits, etc. is a key part to the awareness that we need as witches. The acknowledgment of the "now" can help to ground this experience and bring a deeper awareness to what is happening in the moment that you need to be paying attention to.

In my experience, I have noticed the more I am able to find moments of meditation, concentration, stillness, and finding that connection with the "now" moment, my intentions become a lot clearer. Manifesting also becomes easier and my intuition becomes more viable. Using the exercise of walking around our space and acknowledging every piece that we have added to our tools is, in a way, its own meditation and we can use this exercise in other facets of our lives to bring around our ceremonial practice and bring metaphysical energy into daily tasks. When practicing this, we want to be cognizant that we are not performing these actions for a specific outcome as this can become compulsory. Creating ceremony shouldn't necessarily be because we'll get something more than what it's here for. Pulling ourselves out of the mindset of "magic is for only when we want something" will lessen the potency of your actions. Think of it as that person who only calls when they want something… don't be that witch.

# Chapter Three

*...Never expect or strive for perfection. You are already perfect for this moment.*

Imagine yourself around a fire, cauldron of herbs, potions, and your grimoire in hand. You come to the moment that you need to harness your power. To speak the incantation, for the earth to split beneath you and your dreams will be reality!

Then, you feel an itch on the back of your leg, the neighbor's dog starts barking and your cell phone rings.

A break in concentration can sometimes make your craft feel less impactful, disorganized, and overall less "magical". Although your intention is always the main driver of your endeavors, it's possible that we can feel like we're losing momentum when we feel otherwise distracted from the task at hand.

In the fast-paced environment of modern-day life, we tend to dismiss the idea that we can develop and train ourselves over a period of time to increase our attention, focus, and patience. This isn't to discount or replace the very real help that modern medicine can lend, and it will never be suggested that a magical practice is dulled or incomplete because of its use.

Modern medicine is in fact ancient healing magic when used wisely and with confidence. When we've taken into account the methods we have in place, and we're still feeling like we're falling short in our focus, however, we can add a meditation practice. Stay with me here, as I know that term can immediately elicit groans and eye rolls. I was a yogic educator at one time after all and leading meditation sometimes felt like pulling teeth.

We think that this term, "meditation" means sitting in a seated pose on a pillow, completely still, and not thinking of anything. Not only is that an inaccurate representation of meditation itself, as meditation is incredibly multi-faceted, but the physical demand of this idea is not always accessible to every-body. The practice of meditation, in the simplest of terms, is the focus, acknowledgment, and realization of something. That something can be a word, an item, or a moment. In order to physically accomplish this focus, it's important for the body to feel comfortable, relaxed, and in a neutral, non-stressful position. There are many ways we can practice meditating. I choose to do a lot of my meditation using a focus, whether it is a sound, a rhythm, voice guided (which I teach a lot of), or if it's something as simple as a phrase. Anytime I am making something, black salt for example, there is a moment where I'll put my hands around my bowl, and I'll focus my energy on it. That's an intentional meditation practice. I am focusing and honing in on the task at hand. Bringing myself directly into the present moment brings more potency, intention, and potential success in the outcome.

It takes, on average, 30 consecutive days to create a habit. It will also take just about that entire 30-day period to feel and notice the changes that habit can create in your life. If you're anything like me, my attention can sometimes be all over the place (which is why I really value these meditation practices) so at first, this was a very challenging task. However, I can guarantee that it's worth it in the end, especially when it comes to the various topics being discussed. The amount of "calm and cool" I've been able to elicit in times of stress, specifically those bangs, creaks, or movements while on investigations, or when I'm crafting something that's a more rigorous and concentrated process is far more common than when I first stepped into this line of work.

The earliest records of meditation come from the Upanishads (a Sanskrit word that coincidently translates to, "sitting down near"), ancient Vedic texts written around the 5th century BCE that later inspired the basis of modern Hinduism and are used throughout yogic practices and education (believe it or not, yoga has very little to do with all those intimidating poses. Western culture just didn't get the message). Though we generally know the historical roots of it, we see meditation in practice on a global scale across numerous belief systems. It's easy to draw the conclusion that there is validity to the claims of the practice if one can commit to the path of learning.

Why is meditation so intimidating? Aside from how we think it's practiced, the idea of being alone with ourselves can be more daunting than we realize. When living in such a fast paced, distracting, capitalist society, disassociating almost becomes second nature. We ignore our exhaustion, mental health, as well as our spiritual and emotional needs more often than not. The idea that we might encounter all those thoughts and considerations can create a level of fear that pushes us further away from wanting to truly find mindfulness beyond a surface acknowledgement of it. This fear though, is the very reason why it's so important as it stems from a subconscious concern of knowing that work needs to be done. It's ok to give yourself patience and to nurture yourself into a safe place to explore this side of your spirit. This process is a small part of a deeper spiritual journey known as "shadow work". I truly believe it can help with creating more patience, further developing our critical thinking skills and an objective mindset, which in turn, can immensely help an intuitive practice. An important goal of starting a practice, should include empowerment, stability, and healing on your new path.

I've come across several techniques of starting meditation that often suggest creating a "calm and quiet space" for yourself in order to begin. However, following the path of inclusion, this isn't a reasonable ask for most. Instead, try utilizing a tactic I often teach with where we designate a meditation object. This is something you can hold, wear, or have on your person when you are practicing. By doing this, we are creating a trigger object, if you will, to elicit a meditative mindset when we otherwise might not have access to a physical meditative space. The key to designating your object, is to only use it when you are committing to your moment of meditation. In time, your brain will associate your item, with settling into that mindset. Think of it as the opposite process of breaking a habit, like a rubber band around the wrist. We want to instead invoke the habit. Sleep studies have shown that getting up out of bed when you are unable to sleep will help with rewiring your brain to only associate your bed with sleep instead of restlessness.

Your object is up to you, it can be something as obvious as a set of prayer beads, a special sweater or scarf, a blanket, or a stuffed animal. It can even be a piece of jewelry, a ring, bracelet, hat, or maybe even a book. Believe it or not, starting meditation by settling in for an amount of time to read first is a great start for those who have very restless minds! The possibilities are endless! Just make sure the item you choose is only used for this meditation practice going forward or until you feel comfortable and confident to channel this energy without it.

Here's a simple practice to exercise your mindfulness and meditation technique:

*Once you've settled in, focus on your breath. Count down from 20, assigning a number to each inhale and exhale. When you get to 0, take a moment, acknowledge how you're feeling, where your focus is, and you can decide here if you want to repeat the countdown, raise your number by 10, or if you are finished.*

Don't expect or even strive for perfection. We're performing an action to elicit a habit, that will eventually get easier, more useful with application, and more fruitful as you practice.

When you're finished with this exercise, find a safe place for your item until next time. Setting aside at least 5-10 minutes a day is sufficient to begin the process of creating a habit. Once this is second nature, you'll find making time for meditation becomes easier, and more of a priority. It's so often I hear witches stressing out about making time for their daily craft. Making things like this a habit will, in turn make the daily craft more obtainable.

Whenever I get push back about meditation, whether it's too difficult, hard to focus, etc. I note that our sleep state is just a less controlled and unintentional form of meditation. So why not capitalize on that, and perhaps get an even more restful night? Using the time, we take anyway before bed and creating an intentional process or ritual to it is another way, we can begin to add a conscious practice of mindfulness to our lives and in turn, our craft.

You'll want to set aside the same amount of time asked for your breath awareness, 5-10 minutes, to set your space. We want this to feel more like ceremony with incorporating a new practice into something we otherwise do every night anyway.

This technique is more about what happens before we go to bed than the sleep itself.

If you don't have a specific routine at nighttime, this is the perfect time to start! You can make a checklist, hang it on your bathroom mirror, bedside table, or anywhere you often find your attention. Include therapeutic practices such as 20 seconds of tapping (also referred to as EFT, or psychological acupuncture), brushing your hair or giving yourself a scalp massage. We all know there are times, depending on our daily schedules, where this decompressing time seems unreasonable or unobtainable. Especially those who work 3rd shift, sporadic shifts or multiple jobs. However, by picking up a (this) book that details ways in which you can begin adding daily practice to your life, the want is there. Give yourself patience and grace. Change is uncomfortable and takes time. We can continue to remind ourselves about the cycle we must honor with our growth and journey. Everything will have a beginning, a lifespan, and an end...or transition to something new. When we can embrace these changes during our own transitions, we can bring more awareness and understanding to that discomfort.

When you find yourself settled in bed, find a word, phrase, or mantra. Something you can continuously say out loud or in your head while you calm your mind for sleep. Find something you connect with and repeat until your mind relaxes.

*I welcome peace and stillness into my body*
*I welcome peace and stillness into my mind*
*I welcome peace and stillness into my spirit*

This won't be the last time I repeat the phrase; never expect or strive for perfection. You are already perfect for this moment. You are exactly who and where you need to be for the things that are coming to you and are around you. This idea is not for our past trauma or trying situations, just for this exact moment. It's everything it needs to be. The only thing that matters now, is what we do next.

Speaking of love and light, that brings me around to our second "distraction" that I see amongst the spiritual communities. The idea we can will our traumas away, "love and light" ourselves into happiness, and neglect the work that really needs to be done within ourselves to find peace. We can refer to this as, toxic positivity and we want to avoid it at all costs. There is a time a place for positive thinking. However, there's a fine line of discernment from productive positivity, and disassociation from reality.

The world of witchcraft is there for the fallen, the outcasts, the hurt, and the broken. We are here to find power, healing, peace, and happiness. This path isn't easy, and it's not supposed to be. Energy cannot be created nor destroyed, so to change our own energy, it must transition into a new form. In science, that can mean immense amounts of heat, pressure, speed, time, etc.

It doesn't just change because we think it should or because we want it to. You can touch the universe, but you must also be here for the work and stay vigilant on your journey.

# Chapter Four

*Trauma is not meant to teach you...*

Protection practices and cleansing also create a magic forward life that allows you to play an active role in creating a safe environment. This is important in not only our homes, but when we're entering spiritually or energetic spaces that might be volatile. This is not to say performing these tasks will protect you from everything. We sometimes make the mistake of thinking we can control everything about the outside world, when a big piece of our journey is simply experiencing this existence. Trauma is not meant to teach you and does not need any kind of gratitude. Sometimes bad shit just happens. For the things we can lay an extra barrier down around though, we have witchcraft.

You know that feeling when you've scrubbed the house from top to bottom, cleaned all your bed linens, your favorite blankets, and even wiped down the ceiling fan? There's magic in that feeling. Cleansing, clearing, and otherwise "washing" a space of the energy gunk that doesn't serve us can feel as fresh as a fresh set of bleached and fluffed cotton sheets. This cleaning is a very important part of your magical existence because when we start to frequent beyond the realms of the normal, not everything we encounter will be good. That's not meant to scare you, but protecting yourself, your energy, and your space is incredibly important on this journey. This is especially important if you're already present in spaces that nurture energy beyond the veil (I'm talking to you ghost and cryptid hunters).

To burn, wash, charge, or salt? This question will come up for you throughout your magical journey and the answer is entirely up to you. Exploring ways we can clean our space, items, selves, and tools will make for a very magic forward existence for a long while!

Burning or smoke cleansing with herbs or incense is a common go to for space, item, and self-cleansing. Unless you have permissions culturally, and have been taught how and why to use white sage, I highly suggest leaving it out of your practice. White sage is deeply rooted in indigenous culture and with the rise in popularity of spiritual practices, the poaching of white sage has become dangerously prevalent. A quick internet search will help is explaining this further, but in the scheme of what to burn, there are so many other less harmful, more accessible, and more appropriate options out there. Some of which you may be able to find in your back yard, pantry, or your local supermarket. My big go-to's that I keep on hand are:

- Rosemary sprigs

- Lavender (sprigs and flowers)
- Bay leaves
- Garden sage
- Cedar

When smoke cleansing a space, first and foremost, do not inhale the smoke directly of any burning herb/incense/paper/ or plant when using the smoke to perform magic. Open your windows and work from the lowest level to the top, as you want to "chase" the unwanted energy out but also give it a means of leaving.

Cleansing a consenting person carries the same concept, except you don't have to worry so much about the window aspect. Work from the floor up and think of their crown, or top of the head as the window out.

When cleansing magical items being used in ceremony or crafts the smoke should be treated as a general cleaning agent. Make sure the smoke fills any receptacles being used as well!

Boiling herbs to create steam can also clear a space without the use of smoke, along with using diluted oils or fresh herbs in a spray bottle or diffuser.

Remember, this is not "smudging" as that is a very specific and very closed practice. We can remind ourselves that with growth and change, we will come across things we once thought were ok, and we find that they are not. Change is growth! How we move forward and what we do next is the most important part of this journey. Not everything will be for us, but thankfully we have a rather extensive world to craft from.

Wash cleansing is exactly what it sounds like. You can wash your ceremonial items, spritz them with moon water, use rainwater, or diluted essential oils can be used here as well. The difference between smoke cleansing and washing is really preference. There are times that I will choose to wash, let's say a mixing bowl if I'm wanting to craft something that's for a very specific purpose or with drastically different ingredients than what I used it for before. Perhaps if you're a water witch, you prefer washing items over other cleansing methods. Always be open and available to try new things to see what you connect with. You may surprise yourself!

One of my very favorite protection items to have on hand is, black salt. Salt is a universal cleansing agent that's use within humankind spans back as far, and probably further, than recorded history. It is an integral element in the diets of humans, animals, and even plants. It was used as currency, trade, and preservation. The term salary comes from the word salt. Over time, it's importance and use made its way into tradition, superstition, and magic. As well as salt preserves, it also protects. Not only does ward off rot and death, but also evil and danger. We overlook how deeply something as simple as salt is intertwined in our existence, but it's woven so deeply into our fabric that it's no wonder it would lend potency to our spiritual existence.

Black salt is taking these already mystic properties and

adding intention and a more direct purpose. By infusing our salt with other herbs, stones, ash, and our energy, we can create something that has personal protection properties for ourselves, our loved ones, or others that may need that layer of safety. The best part about this craft, is that it's fool proof. Since salt already carries the protection, cleansing, and healing properties naturally... it basically neutralizes any bad intention. The only small caveat is using it with banishing spells, specifically in instances where the banishing is in turn for protection. Otherwise, it's a perfect craft for any level of practice. You can find a very basic, very simple recipe for black salt in the back of this book. It also considers our exercise in mindfulness as well since we will use meditation to infuse energy into mixture.

Cleansing and clearing is something I tend to speak more on than other mystic practices in the paranormal world. Most cases where I'm called to clear a space for a client, it's often to calm a fear of either activity, experiences, or just that general "spooky" feeling in a home. Helping to detach our physical world from the energy that is unseen, but not unfelt is the most common reason we reach for burning herbs in a space.

So how much more important is it for folks that voluntarily put themselves in those spaces, intent on creating, recording, and experiencing activity? Pretty important. Sometimes that can be lost on spirit seekers because we can often be naturally fearless, skeptical, and occasionally ego driven. However, if we can have and embrace the openness of possibility that there are ghostly apparitions, multi-dimensional existences, and otherwise unexplainable things in this world, what is stopping us from taking every precaution possible in protecting ourselves? There are tools in witchcraft that we can use to proactively protect both before and after investigations.

Our equipment as investigators comes in direct contact with the evidence we look to document and thus sometimes in direct contact with the energy we're investigating. Electronics clearly have energy coursing through them and they're commonly prone to e\affect activity in hauntings. This detail alone should warrant a closer look on how we protect and clear our gear. Best practice is smoke cleansing both before and after entering a space, and always outside of your home. We make sure everything is charged, and ready to go, so adding an additional safeguard can only help protect you and your space. You can pack these items in the same way you pack your gear by adding an herb bundle, crystals, amulets, and any other items to your checklist. Don't forget your torch and a safe place to snuff out any embers!

# Chapter Five

*Humans have been staring at the moon since...*

There is so much imagery in the different sects of witchcraft. These symbols, sigils, or signs all play a part depending on how you want to practice. Are you drawn to the pentacle? The Runic alphabet? Tarot? The sigils of deities or the more intentional application of sigils in intuitive magic (generally referred to as "chaos magic"). There is such a plethora of possibilities available that I often suggest new witches find their path slowly and patiently. I mentioned earlier about the harm that can be caused through cultural appropriation in witchcraft. This idea that we can take and use anything we find interesting… and that it will work for us. This entitled mindset can and will always stunt our magical growth. When we mindlessly mimic what we've seen or read about in an entertainment outlet in lieu of listening to the warnings of older communities of practitioners and neglecting to do the research necessary we're not practicing in a way that will further our power. We are instead falling into a distraction that will lead to an emptiness and inauthenticity. When we see the term closed practice, it's wise to heed the warning. Do the research and take it to heart.

There is so much to explore, practice, learn, and craft from energy that we are welcome to use. Ancient lines of power that are waiting for us to tap into lest we get distracted from them. When we are put into the vessels we are in now, these bodies, they come with a rich history and lineage. Although we are all connected in time, energy, universe, and soul, the bodies we occupy right now are the ones we're here to learn with. These vessels are to be experienced in an inclusive way, to love all, to see past our differences, and to fight and demand equality on a social basis. But our magic, culture, rituals, and practices should be sacred, respected, and honored. I will protect, uplift, fight for, and love my Voodoo sisters and brothers, Santeria sisters and brothers, Indigenous sisters, and brothers, etc. but I will not take sacred and closed practices as my own, as that magic is not meant for me in this time and in this vessel.

Intuitive witchcraft is finding your true path not because it makes you feel unique, special, different, or worthy. But because it's right. You already ARE unique, special, different, and worthy long before the idea of starting or restarting your craft was put into your path.

There are plenty of neutral ways to start a scheduled, ritualistic practice as you settle into your intuition, learn more about your cultural traditions, and eventually allow your methods to grow and blossom around you. One such way that I find to be the most accessible and inclusive, is the lunar cycle.

Humans have been staring at the moon since... Well, since humans have existed. There is a scientific "magic" to the presence of the moon when it comes to how our earth orbits the sun. Without our moon as a sort of stabilizer, it could very well threaten the development of life on this planet.

On a less dramatic scale, the moon controls the tides, the oceans, migrations, and navigation of animals, even the coral in the great barrier reef rely on moonlight to spawn. Our moon's gravitational pull that dictates the changing tides is the strongest around the full and new moon phases. With humans being 70% water, it's no wonder we find heightened emotional changes around this time. If you are a person with a uterus who has a menstrual cycle, you can even find synchronicities between the lunar cycle and your own. Connecting with the lunar cycle in some way gives so many opportunities for intentional magic, crafts, divination, manifestation, cleansing, and more.

The main "phases" of the moon are typically the full moon, new moon, quarter moons, waning/waxing gibbous, and waning/waxing crescent moon phases. We can use the time between each phase for more planned and scheduled daily activities to ramp up the energy and power for the next phase. Depending on what your intention is, the cycle you're working with can be anywhere from 15-30 days. Things like manifesting, growth, and goal setting can perhaps start on a new moon and work until the full moon. If you want to find consistency in your practice or do something that requires the 30 days needed to start a habit, it's useful to work an activity for a complete phase cycle of the moon (new to new, full to full, quarter to quarter, and so on). These longer periods of phase work can be facilitated and organized greatly with a special calendar, journal, or perhaps your grimoire.

The type of magic under each phase varies, but they relate to the path that the moon is taking, so they are very easy to work with and a great practice for new witches or witches that need that more regular focus. I personally identify as a lunar focused witch, with a seasonal flair.

As for the phases themselves, and the magic within each, we can break down the major phases into eight (with a bonus), starting with the new moon.

*N*ew moons are sometimes hard to connect to and work with because they are typically absent from the sky. This phase is created by the alignment of the moon between the earth and the sun. So, we don't see the illuminated side, as it's facing away from us. We can take this phase in a sense of beginning, cleansing, resetting, and starting over. It is fantastic for planning new ventures, manifesting, creating jars or talismans for luck or growth. Think "New Moon, New You" kind of energy (while keeping in mind we don't want to harbor those destination addiction tendencies while manifesting). This is also just as great of a time to allow yourself to be the priority of the moment. Focus on yourself, as the new moon is simultaneously the beginning and the end of the full lunar phase, realize that you are too the beginning and the end of this particular existence, and there is great power in that acknowledgment.

Waxing crescent is the first leg of the race to a full moon. It's when we get our first glimpses of the illuminated face, and we can allow our goals, manifestations, ventures, and growth start to root in possibility. Waxing phase has a focus on "increase" as the moons face in increasing in visibility. Anytime during a waxing moon, we can focus on productive magic or anything that needs momentum and time to build. New friendships, money jars, goal setting, or starting that new habit can all find success while the moon is waxing.

The first quarter moon doesn't mean seeing a quarter of the face, but rather it's taken a quarter of the month cycle to get to this point. Here we see the right half of the moon illuminated while the other half is still cast in shadow. This shows us that we too must be objective about our lives, see both sides of the coin and embrace both the dark and the light, good and bad, success and failure of our plans. Even though we can create magic, find meaning, and manifest the life of our dreams, we still must lay the groundwork and foundation for those walls to be strong and formidable. Be observant and receptive during the first quarter moon, finding crafts that revolve around mindfulness and creativity are great here. Making herb bundles, art, or practicing your meditation can prove fruitful during this phase.

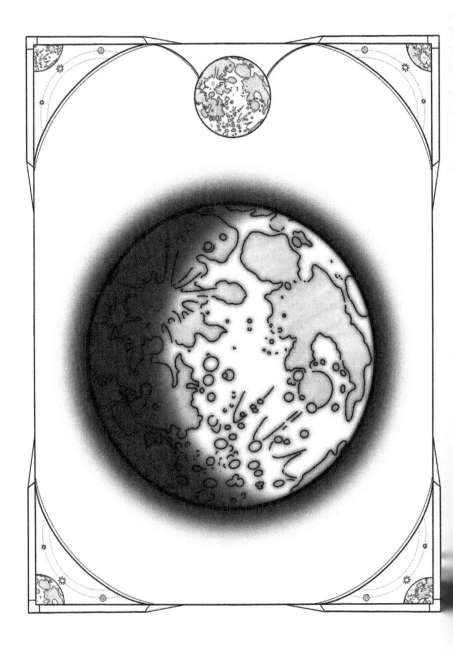

Waxing gibbous is when we see the moon swelling towards its full phase. Gibbous meaning anything that is larger than half, so this is typically when the moon has that football shape to it, or perhaps the shape of an open eye, thus reminding you to keep your eyes open. Be flexible, and open to the developments of your new moon work. If you practice divination (oracle cards or other reading modalities) give yourself a simple reading, single draw to reaffirm your path. Set plans for your full moon ritual, and remember, that even acknowledgement, self-care, and sometimes rest is ritualistic.

The full moon, we all know and love, is most often the phase used in occult imagery, when we can see the full face of the moon. This is often when we think of things like Halloween, werewolves, or people acting strange, but as a witch, this phase gives a big bump to all your magical endeavors. Great for manifesting big energy, prophecy, divination, cleansing and healing. Any crafting, journaling or healing activities that help spiritual development, connect you closer to the universe, or deities, and further develop your magical skill and knowledge are all activities perfect for a full moon. The key words to remember here are abundance and growth. Typically, you can practice under full moon energy for two additional days, the day before the moon is completely full, and the day after.

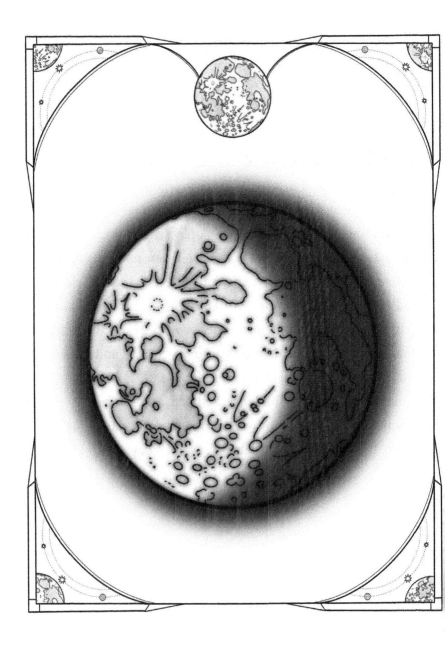

Waning gibbous, the waning moon is when the illuminated face of moon starts to decrease from view before it reaches the third quarter. This is the time to reflect on the abundance of the full moon and set your intention for the inner work. Introspective observation is at hand. Taking mental note of your emotional state, spiritual connection, and setting plans for clearing out the energy within you that is no longer needed or no longer serving your purpose, journey, or path.

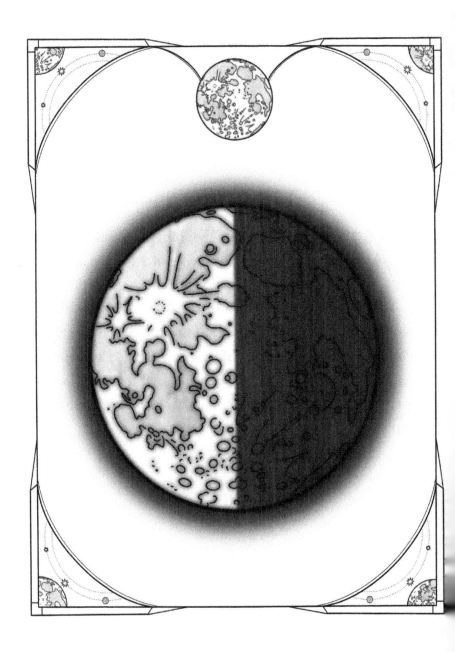

Third quarter much like the first quarter, we are reminded of the dual message that light and dark share power with balance. Now is the time for meditation, journaling, and writing out your plan for releasing the old. Be honest with yourself, as we reach inward into the shadow power of the dark side of the moon to safely reveal the pieces of ourselves that need attention, healing, and release. Set your intentions for your new moon rituals during this phase. Since the new moon has a major focus on our deep shadow health, your plan should include rest and reset.

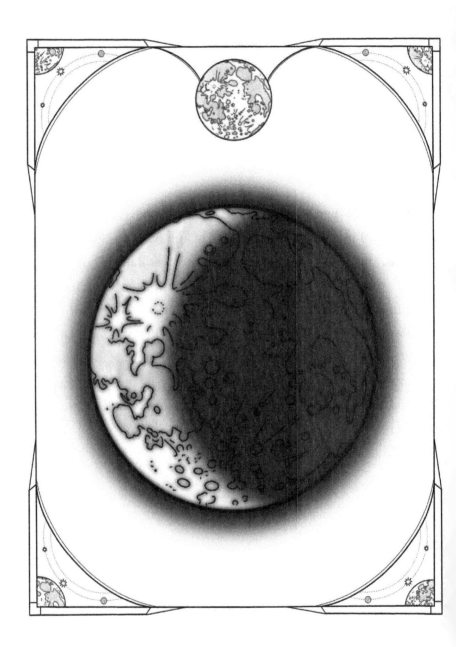

Waning crescent is a crucial time for surrender. Think removing unwanted energy, releasing old habits, or turning inward to our psychic abilities, wisdom, third eye conditioning. This is a great time for kitchen and herb magic. Creating nourishing teas, meals, and feeding your body with intention and love helps us to find that connection with our spiritual body. This physical vessel is just allowing us to occupy earthly space, don't focus on its material presentation to others as they are not on your journey. You are.

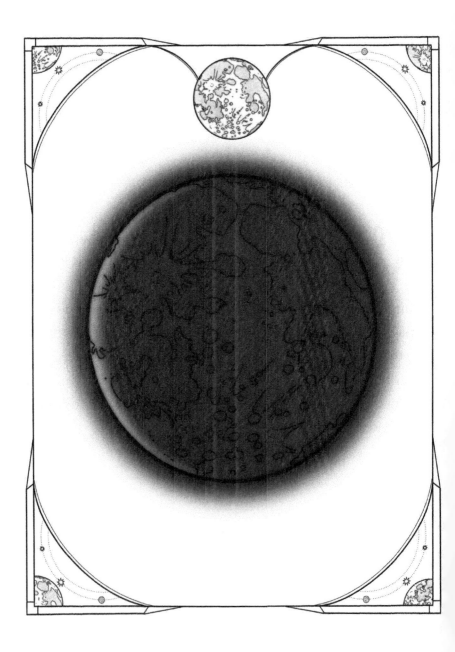

Like the additional days around the full moon, there are some bonus magical times around the new phase as well. The day before that new phase, we have a moment, where there is one last tiny sliver of her light in the sky. Call this the dark moon. It's the last moment of transition for the cycle is complete and we embrace the darkness and stillness that the absence of the moon in the sky brings us. This phase is chock-full of energy we can harness for protection. It's also potent for introspection, shadow work, and deep cleansing rituals. Aside from rest, you can also make potent black salt under a dark moon.

**D**on't feel limited with what you can do under lunar cycles. All magic can be performed whenever you feel it necessary. Think of adding lunar timing to organize and energize more tailored work or to bring different intentions to the same craft. Something like Black Salt can be extra powerful for protection when made under a new or dark moon. It can also provide some extra defense in full moon work, along with the other phases. When we're trying to unlock intuitive crafting, trial and error works well here. You'll never know what works for you, until you practice often, keep good notes, and don't give up. A great place to start is tracking each phase and planning an activity around it. The activity doesn't have to feel magical at first. Maybe it's a cleaning ritual, a special meal, taking time to sit and draw or write, or any other activity that brings you peace, happiness, and ignites your wellbeing. A moonlit walk under a full moon, stargazing under the new moon, taking a bath with Epsom salts and lavender during the waning phase or starting a small and obtainable project around your house during the waxing moon (that you plan to finish by the full moon).

# Chapter
# Six

*...A constant reminder that the cycle never ceases.*

In addition to working with lunar phases, we can align our work with the seasons as well. In time, with the right organization and planning, we can even combine these events to further deepen our practice. The seasons are typically designated as equinox and solstice events. Equinox being when the sun crosses over the earth's equator giving day and night equal lengths in both the northern and southern hemispheres. Solstices occur when the sun has reached its maximum or minimum position away from the equator, causing either the longest or the shortest day/night in the year. These events happen four times annually, two equinoxes and two solstices, and also mark the beginning of each seasonal change. The dates are typically the same every year, but sometimes might vary, so it's always best to check and mark them in your calendar. I deeply associate the seasons with the cycle of life that I often find myself talking about. Honoring that cycle throughout our earth's progression through its own phases allows us to acknowledge and learn with a constant reminder that the cycle never ceases.

The spring equinox happens typically on the 20th of March and represents birth and beginnings. This is when life is bursting forth after a long moment of stillness and rest. The hemisphere awakens and it's as if we have a renewed purpose.

Spiritually, spring is ripe for beginnings in our own lives. Whether it's starting new life changes, projects, ventures, or making big decisions, we often associate these actions with the new year, when instead spring is actually the perfect time for manifesting, planning, and conjuring change and growth in our life. Magic for renewal and growth, starting a Grimoire, or creating a new ritual is perfect for celebrating the representation of birth and beginnings.

The summer solstice happens around the 20<sup>th</sup> or 21<sup>st</sup> of June and represents sustaining life force. It's where we settle into our cycle. This is when humans and animals alike are more active generally. The sun has longer moments in our sky, plants are growing more abundant, and our world seems to be a buzz of activity, because it is.

Check in with yourself and the path you are on during the summer months. Stand firm in your power, reaffirm those activities, hobbies, changes, or decisions you set the groundwork for in the spring and find momentum. The time for abundance is now. Take this time to connect with the magic of nature, this is also the perfect season for outdoor lunar magic, bonfire herb burning, and grounding magic.

utumn equinox, happens around the 22nd or 23rd of September. This is when we begin to slow down. We learn the beauty in endings, we find peace with the prospect of letting go and contemplate the concept of death. We have this fear and sadness around endings in general. It's so important to feel those emotions, learn from them, and embrace our resilience in enduring as humans. However, we can also lean into the acknowledgment of endings being crucial to creation and growth. Change can be painful, uncomfortable and devastating, but also a necessary piece of renewal.

Use this time to organize the things that are no longer serving your path. We typically know the things we should be letting go of, and autumn holds powerful energy to help with that process. Cleansing, clearing, and protection magic is helpful here. Cord cutting, self-care, and nurturing our spirit will prove beneficial. Keep in mind, not all change, cleansing, and growth needs to feel painful. Sometimes the things we need to let go will come with liberation and strength. In time, making space in our lives will encourage creation in ways that we can influence and manifest. We just need to make space first.

The winter solstice occurring on the 21st or 22nd of December represents the stillness that happens after death. We see death as this ultimate finality. Although this is true for these vessels and this journey, it occurs symbolically around us every day. Whether in the seasons themselves, relationships, jobs, emotions, interests, or lifestyles. When we change, develop and grow, we must allow the old to die so that we can make space for new. Winter solstice is about laying to rest all that we've released and removed from our space and allowing stillness to create fertile ground for the abundance of creation. Often looked at as the rebirth of the sun, we experience our longest period of night on the solstice. With that darkness, we can remind ourselves that light also needs rest but it will always come back again.

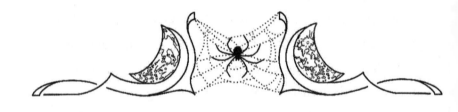

Keeping notes when you practice is a very important detail to find what works for you. Think of it as writing your own recipe book. You'll have a lot of scribbles, torn pages, and rewrites, but make sure you have a record! This is sometimes referred to as a grimoire or a spell book. A notebook of all your magical recipes, rituals, notes, and crafts. Grimoires will grow, change, and develop over time. You may end up with a bunch of ever developing books of your activities and that's wonderful. Makes sure you cleanse and protect each whether through magical means or a good hiding space. Your grimoire should work in tandem with your journal. Your journal is for recording plans, current states of being, spiritual development, your thoughts, and emotions. Grimoires are for creation, while journals are for release. If you're someone who struggles with writing things down, you can keep digital records on your phone, a voice recorder, or a computer/laptop. Using something that works for you is such a crucial part of connecting with your craft.

We are individuals, completely different, unique, and separate from each other. Your craft will not look or be practiced exactly like anyone else's, and that's a good thing. If energetic work was all the same, we wouldn't have the universe. To think this is a one size fits all path is such a limiting mindset. Be respectful, receptive, open, and willing to become part of the fabric of this world but always remember. You are the only witch like you.

Recipes

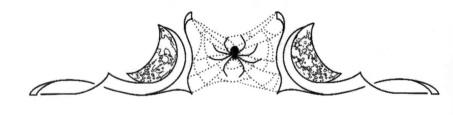

The following recipes, crafts, methods, and ways of doing work are not in any way set in stone. They are just one way of starting a simple practice. Magic develops, it becomes personal, it changes and grows with the practitioner. Think of these activities as just the beginning. Remember, cleanse everything before you begin your recipe. You always want to work from a clean slate without any residual energy on any of your items. When working with fire, be mindful of your surroundings. Make sure the surface you're working on cannot catch fire, don't practice near flammable things like billowy curtains, long hair, furry familiars, flowy sleeves, etc., and have a bowl of water on hand in case your magic gets out of hand. Magic isn't perfect. "Messing up" isn't going to curse your family. These activities are all things that you can learn and grow with, and they don't require perfection. Your focus and intention are paramount. Allow yourself to connect with what you're doing and explore where it takes you.

May they serve you well.

# Basic Items for Your Witchy Pantry

Building a collection of useable items isn't necessary but can be helpful to inspire and give us the means of bringing our magic into a daily routine without needing to always run to the store for your next ritual. Most items we can find at a discount, "everything is a buck" kind of place, and in my opinion, those are really the absolute best places for supplies! If you have the extra cash, and the extra space, some of my must haves (and things you can also use for the following activities) are:

- Candles of all shapes and sizes (stick, jar, and tealight). White and black are always good go to colors as they're universal, but color doesn't necessarily matter at all unless you're using it in your intention.
- Matches, lighters, lighter fluid
- Notebooks, journals, sketch pads with plain white paper
- Pens, Pencils, Crayons, Markers
- Glass jars and containers of all sizes (I've found some amazing mini vials for wearable protection charms)
- Cotton string/twine
- Incense (avoid any "white sage" bundles, as most mass-produced white sage is likely poached or fake and again, we want to avoid harmful practices)
- Baskets or boxes to keep items safely tucked away

- Ceramic mixing bowl (ceramic in case you're adding anything that might be lit like burning paper, herbs, etc.
- Stock pot (best cauldron ever!)
- Dried herbs, salt

There are many magical uses for the dried herbs you may just have on hand in your kitchen or pantry. I urge you to take inventory and do a little research on the seasonings that you were drawn to. I can confidently say there are magical properties for most things in your spice cabinet. Even that packet of taco seasoning. I won't be going into detail about herbal craft, as a witch's herb garden tends to be extensive. Simplicity is sometimes needed when we're forging a new path for ourselves and there are so many amazing books on herbal witchcraft specifically by practitioners who know far more than I do on the subject.

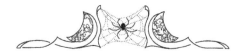

# Protecting Your Grimoire

Whether you are just starting or already have an established practice, you will eventually have so many grimoires you won't know what to do with them all. I personally have a scratch pad grimoire, pocket grimoire, decorative grimoire, grimoires for dark and light style magics, etc. The good thing is, there are no set rules in that department, so figure out what works for you organizational wise and go with it! My only strong advice when it comes to keeping a book of your crafts is, keep it as safe as possible. These books can be incredibly personal and just like anything else in our lives, extra safeguard never hurts. One way I like to keep my books safe from prying eyes is a little protection spell in the first few pages. This can be a poem style, a sigil or symbol, a smear of black salt, or anything that makes it feel safe to you. I'm very partial to rhyming in my work, (I know that's a witch trope, but I really can't help it.)

This craft will walk you through setting up a simple circle to safely bind your grimoire with protection.

Ingredients:
- Notebook or journal that you'll be using as a grimoire
- Salt
- A clean surface to work on that gives you the ability to gather your salt back up to reuse later
- A permanent writing utensil (pen or marker)

- A candle
- Cleansing method of choice
- An arm's length of cotton twine (enough to wrap your book once and tie a bow or lose knot)

Optional items:
- Some black salt
- A sprig of dried rosemary, lavender, or garden sage

Create a safe circle to work. This can simply be a line or sprinkle of salt around your area, smoke cleansing the area before you begin, or any additional preparatory practice you may have in place. For this recipe, we'll be sprinkling salt on the surface that we're working on and, of course cleansing all our ingredients before we begin.

When you are ready, light your candle and take a moment of reflection and meditation. Imagine an iron clad room or a fortress that has unscalable walls. Keeping this imagery in your mind open your grimoire to the first page and write your poem, sigil, symbol, or otherwise protective mark on the inside. Close your book and wrap your twine around it and tie a bow or loose knot, while doing this, you could recite your poem if you wrote one, otherwise you can say something like:

"Protect this book from prying eyes, hearts of cold, and deceitful spies.
Let scheming glances go unfulfilled, for the secrecy of my work

is within my power and of my will"

There are a few options you can take with your string or twine. Water cleanse it for your next protection ritual, but make sure its dry before storing it safely. Use repeated ingredients like this for similar or same rituals as in only use this particular cut of twine when doing protection spells on your grimoires and journals. This can help with binding the spells together and increasing the potency of the overall protection among your writings! You can also burn your twine to bind that magic by fire. The soot created can be used to mark the front and back of your book, or you can bury it, put it in a plant, or perhaps mix it with ink, and write your incantation on the inner pages. Be sure that the remnants are further used to strengthen your craft, and not for other means or in other spells.

As a note when it comes to how you're keeping track of your spells, thoughts, and personal notes; if you use a computer, your phone, or any other electronic item, you can modify this craft to suit your needs. Be careful with using water and salt close to any openings or outlets. Otherwise, magic develops and grows with us, even with the advances we have now as modern-day practitioners.

# Notes

# Black Salt

Ingredients:

- Sea Salt – Table salt also works just fine
- A piece of paper and writing utensil
- Candle
- Matches
- Stick of incense or your favorite smoke cleansing herb (burnable cleansing is important here)
- Fireproof bowl (any heavy Stoneware, ceramic, glass bowl will work. No plastic!)
- Something to stir around your items
- Airtight jar or container to keep your salt for future use

Optional Extras

- Mortar and pestle to create a finer salt
- Additional herbs (lavender, basil, and dead nettle are great for protection spells)
- Charcoal cakes – helps with burning your intention paper, any herbs you want to smoke cleanse with, and makes your salt a deeper color
- Crystals to add when you're done making your salt – I'll add quartz chips if I'm making charms to wear as it can act like a battery that helps to strengthen the protection properties when I'm investigating those extra creepy places.

Always start your craft with intention. This is where our mindfulness comes in handy, we want to be focused, present, and connected to what we're doing. Remember, salt is naturally cleansing and neutralizing, so this is a perfect way to practice your intention and focus. Cleanse all your ingredients, tools, self, and space. You can do this by waving your smoke cleansing of choice working first from your feet to your head, then from the floor up in your workspace, and ending with each item including inside of any jars or receptacles.

I light myself a candle after cleansing and before beginning my work. This is, in a way, a signal of my beginning, and I can allow myself to let go and disconnect when I blow the candle out at the end. I like to create this idea of honoring the cycle (birth, life, death) in most of my work. The candle represents that cycle here. Plus, it's helpful to burn needed items as well!

Add your ingredients to your mixing bowl in order; salt, charcoal cake if using, and any additional herbs. While everything is "marinating", take your paper and writing utensil and write your protection intention, what you might be protecting yourself against if for a specific purpose, or maybe a power word, phrase, or any sigils or symbols (details on sigil writing can be found in the next recipe).

Fold this paper away from you, 3 times, this again is preference. I work a lot in threes (birth, life, death, remember?) so the number is prevalent in my work. However, you may have another power number, 7, 9, etc. Use what you are called to, but still fold away from yourself since we are working to repel energy that we don't want in our lives. Then, burn it. By burning things in our practice, we're theoretically doing a few things; sending it to another realm in some cases, activating it with fire, or in this case, changing its chemical makeup to then be able to infuse our salt with our written intentions.

From here, we want to mix our ingredients together by stirring with whatever we're using to mix, I use a ceremonial dagger, but a spoon, heatproof wand, etc. is equally as perfect.

(At this point you can choose to briefly transfer your salt to a mortar and pestle to make it into a finer product but be sure to put it back in your bowl for the final step.)

Making sure your mixture is back in your bowl, this is where you can "write" sigils or symbols, if you have any, into your sand with your finger or any ceremonial object you might be using. More importantly, take a moment, to pour your intention into your salt. We can use our practice in mindfulness here, but you can also use the following "voice guided" meditation to focus your energy into your craft:

*Imagine a light just above your head, maybe it's a ball of light, maybe it's a halo, however it shows up for you. Imagine that light getting warmer and eventually you bring that light into your body, down the back of your neck, and into your chest. Let it warm up a little in your chest before bringing it into your shoulders, down your arms, and into your hands. Let that warm settle into your palms over your bowl and imagine that light again, pouring from your hands into your bowl. Filling it to the brim with universe energy. When you feel it's complete, allow that light to finish trickling out of your palms, and rub your palms together to signify its completion.*

Finally, the salt can be transferred to your cleansed receptacle(s) (jar, vial, etc.) of choice. If you lit a candle before your crafting, you can blow it out now to end your session. Feel free to re-cleanse if needed, and you have yourself you're a nice jar of protection!

This recipe can used anytime you need a batch of salt. When you start to bring your practice into your everyday, you may find times that you feel more powerful, potent, or drawn to doing work. Pay attention to those feelings. Journaling, marking on a calendar, and keeping notes are all great ways to not only track your patterns, but also helps with accountability and consistency. If you find that you do your best work under a full moon, on Wednesdays, during a certain season, or at sunrise, you can start to incorporate that into a schedule. The goal is to make your craft a habit. An everyday occurrence.

# Intentional Symbols or sigils

"Sigils" from the Latin word meaning "seal", are the written symbols or invocations of spirits or deities. But there's a way to bring these symbols into a more intentional application by creating them with a word, or phrase. By making the symbol this way, you're creating something that you can use, scribe, carve, or draw in your crafts. Whether it's drawing it into your black salt, or above a door frame, the possibilities are endless. One thing I really like about this method of creating symbols is that it's very personal. So, the meaning behind the symbol isn't for anyone other than the practitioner using it. Don't expect to do any damage by putting a mean symbol on someone's birthday card. It's not that easy to practice baneful magic, and that's not what we're here to learn about anyway. The application of this process can be altered and tailored to however you want to perform it. Especially the "secret code" part. So have fun, experiment a lot, and practice every day.

Ingredients:
- Cleansing of choice (always)
- Writing utensil and pad of paper
- Candle and heat/fireproof surface

Cleanse all your items and light your candle. You will first figure out how you want to make your code key, you want to include all the letters of the alphabet and give them numeric values. How you assign them is up to you, but it's best to figure out a code, and stick with it so all your symbols are made in with the same energy and method. For this example, I'm using a simple alpha numeric code:

| A | B | C | D | E | F | G | H | I | J | K | L |
|---|---|---|---|---|---|---|---|---|---|---|---|
| 1 | 2 | 3 | 4 | 5 | 6 | 7 | 8 | 9 | 10 | 11 | 12 |

| M | N | O | P | Q | R | S | T | U | V | W | X |
|---|---|---|---|---|---|---|---|---|---|---|---|
| 13 | 14 | 15 | 16 | 17 | 18 | 19 | 20 | 21 | 22 | 23 | 24 |

| Y | Z |
|---|---|
| 25 | 26 |

Once you've come up with a code you like, lay out a grid, circle, or any simple shape with single digit numbers. Here are two such examples, the possibilities are endless

Now it's time to write your message, invocation, power word, protection statement, etc. Here are some examples, but this is not

limiting you. It's merely to get you started. This craft will grow and develop just like all the ones you will learn on your journey.

"Protect me and my family from those who wish to cause harm"

"Money and wealth are coming to me"

"Protect my home from energy that does not serve me"

And so on.

We'll use this as our example:

*I am confident, creative, and capable*

Make sure your statement is written clearly in one straight line. You'll then want to remove any duplicates of letters to condense the phrase. Make sure this is all done on the same piece of paper, so the original intention is clear (it will start to look a little odd but trust the process).

*I am confident, creative, and capable*

*I a m c o n f d e t r v p b l*

After this step, you will assign each letter to the numeric character in your code and then add double numbers together until they create 1 number per letter.

| I | a | m | c | o | n | f | d | e | t | r | v | p | b | l |
|---|---|---|---|---|---|---|---|---|---|---|---|---|---|---|
| 9 | 1 | 13 | 3 | 15 | 14 | 6 | 4 | 5 | 20 | 18 | 22 | 16 | 2 | 12 |
| | | 1+3 | | 1+5 | 1+4 | | | | 2+0 | 1+8 | 2+2 | 1+6 | | 1+2 |

9  1  4  3  6  5  6  4  5  2  9  4  7  2  3

Repeat the same step of crossing out any duplicates.

9  1  4  3  6  5  6̸  4̸  5̸  2  9̸  4̸  7  2̸  3̸

9  1  4  3  6  5  2  7

For more intricate symbols, it's ok to skip the numeric grid above, and just use all 26 letters of the alphabet to create a grid!

Once you have your "code" it's time to draw. Connect your letters or numbers in order on your grid to create a, sometimes chaotic, symbol. This is your intentional sigil. It's ok if it looks funny, or weird. That's intentional! Sigils and symbols shouldn't look like anything you've seen before. You're creating something new and personal. Embrace the weird.

Write your sigil (in the same stroke order that it was written on your grid) in a safe place for future use or right where you intend to use it. Then you'll burn the paper to "activate" its power. That symbol will still hold intention and power even after your paper is burned, just remember to write it in the same order each time.

To reiterate from the opening of this activity; sigil/symbol writing has MANY methods. This is just one such method that I find easiest to educate with. Find what works for you, and make sure to record your process for future use.

I am Confident, creative, and capable

# Notes

# Manifest/Goals/Protection Jars

Jar magic can be found throughout different practices across the globe. The act of containing items inside a receptacle to create potions, intentions, protection and sometimes even prisons can be found in both history and entertainment when it comes to crafting. One of the earliest documentations of bottle magic dates as far back as 1681, but the craft itself most likely even precedes that timeline in practice.

Popular in North American folk magic, jars are used to concentrate the power of a spell and provide portability of storage or display. You can use any sealable container that relates to the type of spell you're doing, but any jar will do. For this recipe, a jar of any size so long as you can see inside of it will work perfectly. I will even base grocery purchases on the container things might come in so that I can use them later! Since there are so many different and useful herbs, stones, materials, and methods to make jars, have fun exploring and researching ingredients depending on the intention of your craft. I've listed some ideas below to get you started.

The examples used here are only a very small sample of how you can use this method in your work.

General Ingredients:

Manifest/Goal Jar

- Writing utensil
- Small piece of paper
- Candle
- Bay leaf – protection, success, and wishes
- Salt – protection and connection to universal powers
- Cinnamon, clove, or allspice – gives a little kick to your spell. Also good for abundance, luck, and happiness
- Optional crystals – clear quartz, the catch all for magical stones. Citrine, a great stone for abundance

Protection Jar

(Using at least 3 additional ingredients with your black salt helps to make a potent and effective protection jar. For paranormal investigators, these work really nice in your gear in a small pocket-sized receptacle)

- Back salt – personal protection
- Rosemary – protection against negative forces and attitudes
- Lavender – strength and protection
- Bay leaf – protection activated by fire
- Black pepper – protection from evil energy
- Basil – protection from spirit energy
- Optional stones: obsidian, quartz, amethyst are all powerful protection stones

Smoke cleanse all materials, especially your jars!

In a manifesting jar, I will often make a small list of broad goals that I'm manifesting for. If you want to be specific, stick to one focused goal at a time.

For example, I can make a jar for success, luck, and abundance to cover my focused goals of being an author, public speaker, and eventually doing those things for a living. Or I can be more specific by using a short-term goal: Sell 1,000 copies of my book.

You'll find more success with being specific rather than hoping that your magic with spread across the 20-item checkbox list of demands.

When creating a protection jar, the process is similar to creating black salt. Add your ingredients and pour your focus, and power into your jar using the meditation techniques we've discussed.

Sealing your jars with wax is a common practice, but it isn't always necessary. Some jars can be added to, whether it's freshening up an affirmation, putting a penny in a day as an offering, or collecting fire activated wishes by dropping in a burning bay leaf with something written on it.

Otherwise, you can seal your jar with wax of a corresponding color (green for money, red for love, and so on), you can tie twine around the top, you can even use handy dandy duct tape. Whatever you have access to will work. When your jar is complete, you can either display it somewhere safe where you can see it every day, perhaps in a high up spot to allow the magic to spread all over your space, or you can bury it in your yard, garden, or a big potted plant to encourage your magic to grow or to protect your property. The safe keeping of your jar has endless possibilities as jar magic is such an extensive craft.

# Cord Cutting

Cord cutting can be both effective, and a strong symbolic affirmation of growth or commitment to releasing energy, habits, people, and relationships that are no longer serving us. Commonly used to move on from events like a breakups, toxic relationships, or unhealthy situations. Cord cutting can also be a powerful ceremony when we need to move past life events, fears, and other traumas that can rob us of our peace.

Like every craft we do, make sure you cleanse all materials needed before beginning your ritual!

Ingredients:
- Two small stick candles, one representing you, and one representing what you're cutting ties with or moving on from
- Salt or black salt for a ring of protection around your candles
- Fireproof surface to perform your magic (a small plate works)
- Cotton twine, long enough to loosely wrap around both candles
- Small needle or pin to carve into the wax of each candle or a writing utensil for the tea light recipe
- Jar or container that you can store discarded candle remnants for later burning

After cleansing all your items, you'll designate which candle represents you by carving your name or simply "me" on it with your pin. The other candle doesn't need a designation because the act of cutting the cord will aid in you releases what you need to.

Tie the ends of the twine together in order to use it to connect your two candles, you'll want to end up with about 3-4 inches of space between them. *Pro tip, you can lightly warm the wax underneath the twine to adhere it to the candle by breathing a few good "fog the window" breaths where your twine sits.

Using candle holders if needed or slightly melting the bottom of each candle with a lighter to adhere them to your fireproof surface to keep them upright.
Sprinkle a circle of salt around the candles and concentrate on creating a space that holds you, and that which you are releasing, within it.

Then, you will declare that you are cutting the cord between you and whatever you need to separate from before lighting first the candle that represents you, and then the other. Allow the candles to burn. Stay present and observant during this process.

You can choose to meditate, journal, or just be there. Eventually the candles will burn to the twine, and the twine will ignite and separate the two candles. Continue to allow the candles to burn all the way down before blowing them out if they don't extinguish on their own.

The candle representing you should be put in a safe personal space, or it can be buried so that you may grow from this release. The twine can be burned if it didn't burn all the way during your ceremony.

Your other candle can either be burned or perhaps added to a melt pile to make candles for other ceremonies as the other candle generally represented what you needed to separate from and wasn't energetically tied to anything.

## Alternate Single Candle Recipe

If multiple stick candles aren't accessible, this recipe works in the exact same way with one candle. Since the candle itself won't represent anything in this version, you are able to continue using it for other purposes afterwards.

Ingredients:
- 1 candle
- 2 empty cardboard toilet paper rolls (or 1 paper towel roll cut in half)
- 2-3 inches of twine or cotton thread
- Heat/fireproof plate or surface
- Salt
- Scissors

Remember to cleanse all multi use items before and after

each ceremony. You will write your name on the cardboard roll that represents you, and then you can write whatever you are cutting the cord from on the opposing roll, but it's not necessary as the intention is more important. The candle will be placed between the two rolls and the string strung across above it by making a single notch in the top of each roll with scissors to wedge the string into so it will hold for the ritual. Be sure that the candle is a few inches below the string. If using a larger candle, you can always stack your cardboard rolls and string on a couple of overturned bowls, or pots.

After declaring your intentions for the ceremony light your single candle beneath the string. Once the string heats, ignites, and separates, you can use a fireproof pot or receptacle to completely burn the roll representing what you are separating yourself from. Then, bury the roll that represents you so that the earth's energy can help you heal and grow. Keep each end of the string with the individual rolls.

Don't panic if both rolls go up in flames, this is a cord cutting ritual after all and sometimes that cord needs to be cut with some vigor. Be sure you're working on a surface that is fireproof and that you're away from anything that could catch fire. Pro tip: keep a bowl of water, spray bottle, or fire extinguisher on hand for all magic using flame.

We won't always be able to plan ahead for our crafting time. Sometimes we will have gaps in our habits, and it can feel like we need to start over with connecting to our practice again. For this, here are a few small daily crafts that take a few seconds or minutes of your time and will keep that energy and mindset present in your daily life.

## Bay Leaves

Keep a jar on hand when you feel the need to connect or reconnect to your magic. It's as simple as writing a wish, intention, or a powerful word on a leaf and burning it. When we activate this with fire, it goes into the atmosphere surrounding us and can act as a little charge of energy. It can be helpful to hold your bay leaf with a pair of scissors as you burn it rather than trying to hold it with your hands. If bay leaves aren't available, small pieces of paper that you've bulk cleansed work perfectly. Fill a jar with your smoke cleanse of choice and throw your cut up or ripped up pieces of paper in there. Use as needed. Bay leaves are known for being powerful herbs of transformation and manifestation.

## Cinnamon Sticks

Typically, the sticks of cinnamon we see in the grocery store are cassia vera, but they both have the same intention. This is another method of smoke cleansing but with a little spice. I often save burning a stick of cassia when I really need to give myself a jolt of energy. Plus, they burn very slowly so one stick lasts a very long time! Cassie is a potent herb for protection, success, and passion so it's great for lighting a fire when you feel disconnected from your practice.

## Manifesting and Cleansing While Bathing

There is no doubt we can be extremely powerful when we are at our most vulnerable. When we bathe, whether it's a shower, a bath, washing our hands, or even using some hand sanitizer, it's a prime time for incantations. Use some of the phrases below, or create your own and repeat them a few times while you're cleansing:

"My life is abundant in the ways that best serve my highest self."

"I release the things that no longer serve me."

"I am powerful, I am safe, I am loved."

## Moon Gazing

This is something that I use in my personal practice. We will sometimes fall into the mindset that being a practicing witch means doing some sort of ritualistic activity or immersing your time in ceremony, incantations, and jar magic. Moon gazing is a form of meditation that brings us back into our moment. It allows us to let go of the pressure and stress of feeling like we must perform in some way to be a witch. This activity is exactly what it sounds like. Wrap yourself in blankets, grab your journal, telescope, or just indulge in the light of the night sky. Be still and contemplative for at least 15-20 minutes if not longer. A great way to think of this activity is by recognizing that the moon is powerful enough to affect our world in such profound ways, that it can also affect us physically, spiritually, emotionally, and energetically.

In order to manipulate universal energy, we must remember and often be reminded that we are of the universe.

# Notes

There isn't a rule book for all witchcraft. Just like there isn't a rulebook when it comes to living in the world of the paranormal as a whole. There are guidelines, moral standards, things that we do know, and things we have yet to figure out. The idea that these worlds are a one size fits all community isn't something you will ever have to worry about.

To be a witch is more than a declaration. It's a commitment, a practice, and a constant acknowledgement that our world is saturated in mysticism, secrets, magic, and power. In order to discover and develop a relationship with these energies, we must discover and develop a relationship with ourselves.

Be open to exploring your surroundings and trying new things. Be respectful of the communities you want to be part of and get comfortable with failure. Figuring things out will sometimes be met with downfalls, being told no, and learning that not everything can work in your favor. How you grow, develop, and move forward is what truly sets forth your path. These physical bodies are just vessels in the ever-expanding universe and your energy is an ancient force that spans space and time. Don't allow the hiccups, missteps, or failures to stop your growth.

Take a lesson from the universe that you're a part of.

Never stop growing.